## FICTION 🪶 HENRY'S GHOST

Written by Katherine Rawson
Illustrated by Ann Caranci

**Chapter 1**  The Big Kid . . . . . . . . . . . . . . . . . . . . . . . 2
**Chapter 2**  The Flashlight . . . . . . . . . . . . . . . . . . . . . 5
**Chapter 3**  Alone in the Dark . . . . . . . . . . . . . . . . . . 10
**Chapter 4**  What's in the Woods? . . . . . . . . . . . . . . 13

PIONEER VALLEY EDUCATIONAL PRESS, INC.

## CHAPTER 1 — THE BIG KID

"Let's get the camping supplies ready," said Dad. "Tomorrow's the big day."

Luke jumped up from his chair. "I'll get our things out of the basement," he said.

Henry sighed as his big brother headed to the basement. Every summer Dad and Luke went on a camping trip, and every summer Dad said Henry was too young to go with them.

Luke came out of the basement and handed a backpack to Henry.

"What's this for?" asked Henry.

"Didn't Luke tell you?" said Dad.

"Tell me what?" asked Henry.

"You're a big kid now," said Dad. "You're old enough to come with us."

Henry couldn't believe it. This was better than anything he could think of. Better than pizza and chocolate ice cream!

"All right!" he shouted, leaping up and running to hug Dad.

"Calm down there," laughed Dad. "Why don't you take some of that energy and help Luke with the tent?"

"OK!" shouted Henry, and he ran down the basement steps after his brother.

That night, Henry lay awake, thinking about the camping trip. Luke had always told him how much fun it was to fish in the lake, cook over a campfire, and hike in the woods. He couldn't wait to do those things himself.

But then Henry thought about sleeping outside. That would be the hard part. The woods were dark and filled with strange noises and animals.

Henry still slept with a nightlight on. There was no way he could sleep without one. But he couldn't tell anyone that he was afraid of the dark. Luke would laugh, and Dad would say that he was too young to go camping.

# CHAPTER 2  THE FLASHLIGHT

The following morning, Henry looked through a book about camping. The book had tips for starting fires and setting up tents. It also had a list of things to pack for a camping trip. The first item on the list was a flashlight.

"A flashlight!" thought Henry. He wouldn't be scared of the dark if he had a flashlight.

After breakfast, Henry helped pack their gear into the car. He picked up a small flashlight.

"Can I carry this, Dad?" he asked.

"Sure," said Dad. "Why?"

"I just want to be helpful," said Henry.

After a long drive, Dad pulled the car over next to a sign. "Here's the trail," he said.

Dad, Luke, and Henry put their packs on their backs and started down the trail. The sounds of the road grew farther away.

HAPPY TRAIL

"Are we there yet?" asked Henry.

"Not yet," said Dad, and they kept walking. Suddenly, they heard a noise.

"Hoo-hoo-hoo-hoo!"

"What was that?" whispered Henry. He turned on the flashlight, even though it was still light outside.

"Just an owl," said Luke. "Sometimes you hear them in the day."

They came to a small clearing in the woods.

"We'll camp here," said Dad.

Henry helped Dad set up the tent while Luke looked for firewood. It wasn't dark yet, but the sun was starting to set.

"We'll need water to cook our dinner," said Dad. He handed Henry a jug. "Would you go fill this in the spring?"

Henry looked at the field where Dad was pointing. His stomach grew tight.

"You're not afraid, are you?" laughed Luke.

"No!" said Henry, and he headed down the path.

## CHAPTER 3 ALONE IN THE DARK

Henry carried the water jug in one hand and the flashlight in the other. When the fire was out of sight, he turned on his flashlight.

Something rustled through the trees above. Henry looked up but saw only leaves and branches. Suddenly, he heard wings flapping.

"Just a bird," he thought, but his heart pounded.

"Where is that spring?" wondered Henry as he went down the path. It seemed to go on forever.

Finally he spotted a small spring of water in the flashlight's beam. Henry bent down and dipped the jug into the spring.

Then he saw it.

A white shape floated silently through the sky. As it disappeared into the treetops, Henry heard something like a scream.

For a moment, Henry could not move.

Then he turned around and ran, tripping over roots and rocks along the way. He didn't even know if he was on the right path.

At last he saw an orange glow ahead. The campfire! He ran straight for it and saw Dad and Luke.

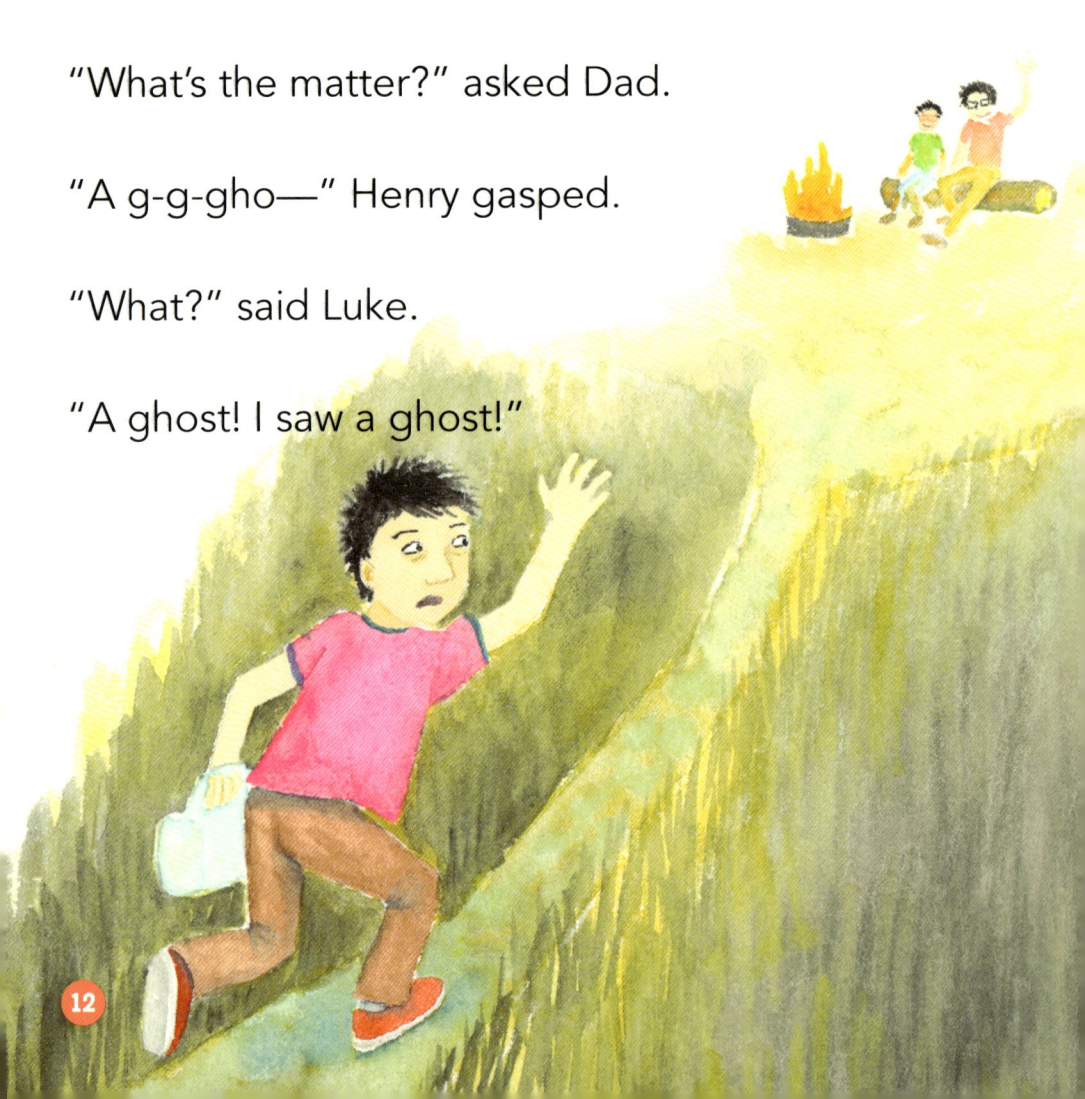

"What's the matter?" asked Dad.

"A g-g-gho—" Henry gasped.

"What?" said Luke.

"A ghost! I saw a ghost!"

# CHAPTER 4  WHAT'S IN THE WOODS?

Luke burst out laughing. "A ghost?"

"I saw it!" said Henry. "It was white with big black eyes, and it was floating. Then I heard something scream."

Dad put his arm around Henry. "I think I know what you saw," he said. "And it's nothing to be afraid of."

"What do you mean?" said Henry.

"It sounds like you saw a barn owl."

"It couldn't be," said Henry. "I didn't hear wings flapping. And it didn't make a hooting noise."

"That's just like a barn owl," said Dad. "People call them ghost owls because they're so white. Come on, I'll show you."

He started down the path toward the spring with Henry and Luke close behind him. They crossed the spring and came to a meadow.

Henry looked around. "What now?" he asked.

"Now we wait," said Dad.

"For what?" asked Henry.

"For the ghost, of course," said Dad.

After a few minutes, Henry saw the white shape floating in the sky. He pointed his flashlight at the shape and saw that it really was an owl. "What's it doing?" he asked.

"Hunting," said Dad. "Since it flies so quietly, the mice can't hear it."

"Why can't we hear its wings flap?" asked Henry.

"Owls have special feathers that help them fly very quietly," said Luke.

Henry switched off his flashlight and watched the owl circle the trees in silence.

Suddenly, the owl let out a sharp cry.
Henry jumped back. "That wasn't quiet!" he said.

"It's calling its mate now," said Luke.

"Nature is full of interesting things," said Dad. "When you learn about them, they aren't so scary."

"I guess you're right," said Henry. But he stuck close to Dad as they walked back to the campsite.

On the way back, Henry heard the owl's cry again. He grabbed his flashlight, but he didn't turn it on. "Just a barn owl," he thought. He could see the light of their fire ahead.

# NONFICTION · BIRD FEATHERS

Written by Katherine Rawson

**Chapter 1**  All About Feathers............18

**Chapter 2**  Look at a Feather............21

**Chapter 3**  The Life of a Feather........ 24

**Chapter 4**  Camouflage..................26

**Chapter 5**  Beautiful Feathers...........29

GLOSSARY .............32

## CHAPTER 1 | ALL ABOUT FEATHERS

When you look at a bird, what do you see? You may see bright colors on its chest. You may see spots on its throat or stripes on its wings. You may see a long, curly tail or a **crest** on its head.

A bird's feathers can tell you a lot about that bird.

crest

Feathers are very important to birds. They can protect a bird's skin. They can also help a bird hide from its enemies.

Birds spend a lot of time **preening** their feathers to keep clean. When birds preen, they remove dirt from their feathers. Preening also covers the feathers with oil to keep them waterproof.

Smaller birds have fewer feathers than larger birds. Some birds grow extra feathers in the winter to keep warm.

Birds are the only living animals with feathers. Some dinosaurs had feathers as well.

# CHAPTER 2  LOOK AT A FEATHER

Feathers come in different shapes and colors, but they are all made of **keratin**. Our hair and nails are made of keratin too.

If you look closely at a feather, you will see a line of keratin down its center.

keratin

A bird can have different kinds of feathers.

## Flight Feathers

Flight feathers grow on a bird's wings and tail. They are strong enough to support a bird in the air.

## Contour Feathers

**Contour** feathers give a bird its color and shape. They are only colored on the edges where they can be seen.

## Down Feathers

Birds also grow soft down feathers. These may be white or gray. Down feathers keep birds warm.

Down feathers keep people warm too! Your pillows or winter jackets may have down feathers inside them.

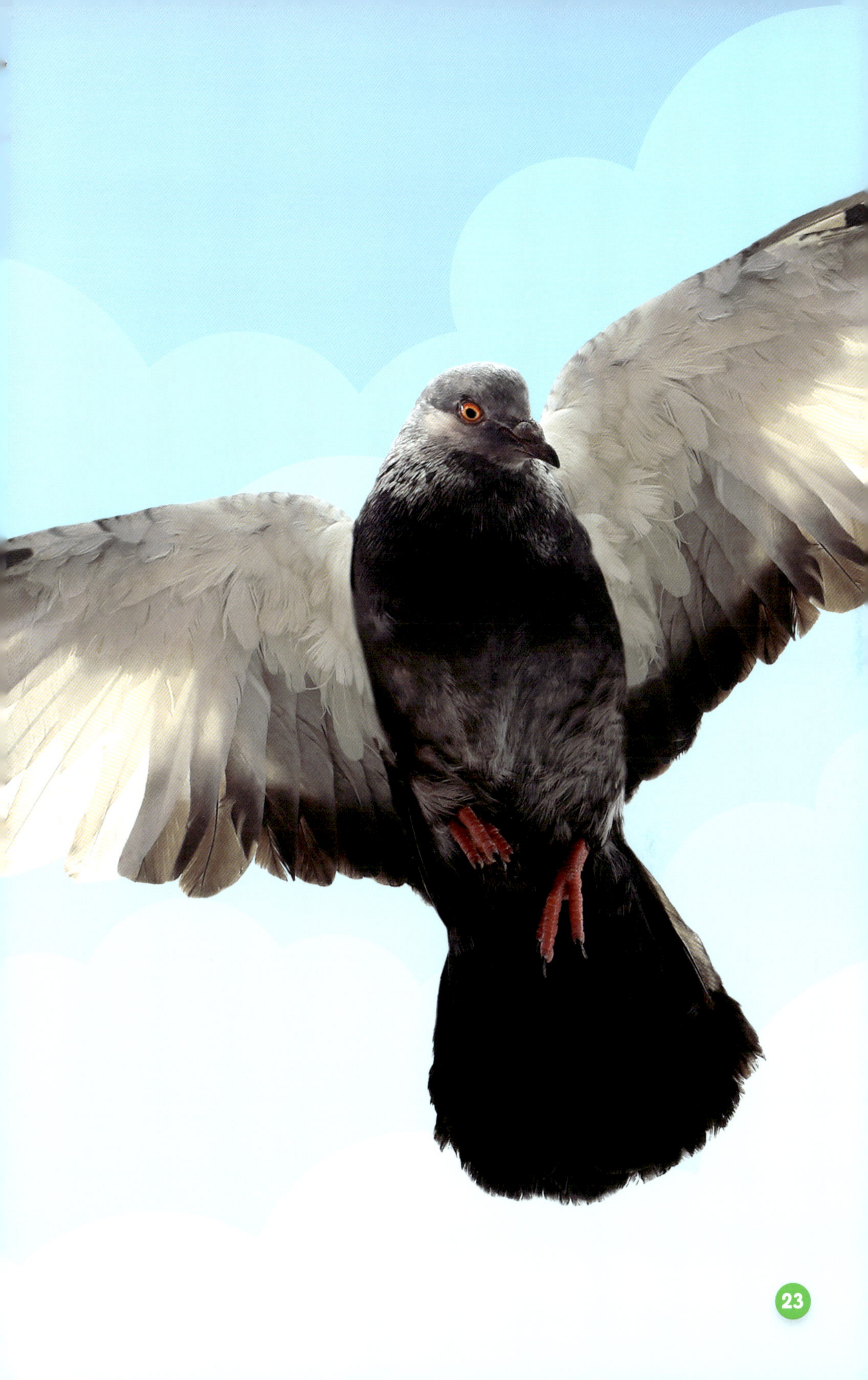

## CHAPTER 3 | THE LIFE OF A FEATHER

Not all birds are born with feathers. Many birds have no feathers when they hatch. Some baby birds are covered with soft down. They stay close to their parents to keep warm until their feathers grow.

The feathers on young birds may be dull, spotted, or striped. This helps young birds on the ground hide from **predators**. Once their adult feathers grow in, they are ready to learn to fly.

Birds do not keep the same feathers for their whole lives. They lose their old feathers at least once every year. This is called **molting**.

When a bird molts, it does not lose all of its feathers at once. It takes a few weeks for the old feathers to fall off. During that time, the new feathers grow in.

## CHAPTER 4 | CAMOUFLAGE

Have you ever seen an owl napping on a branch? You may have passed by one without seeing it. The colors of some owls' feathers blend in with the colors of tree bark. After a night of hunting, an owl can sleep all day in a tree without being seen.

Many birds have colors that blend in with their surroundings. This is called **camouflage**. Feathers that are brown, spotted, or striped can help birds hide in leaves, bushes, or grass. Some birds use camouflage to hide from predators.

Hunting birds use camouflage to sneak up on their **prey**.

Snowy owls have white feathers that blend in with the snow. The female snowy owl has black spots on her white feathers. These camouflage her when she nests.

The ptarmigan (TAR-mi-gan) is another bird with camouflage feathers. Its color changes with the seasons. In the winter, its white feathers blend in with the snow. When the snow melts, the feathers turn brown.

Ptarmigans also grow feathers on their feet. The feathers keep their feet warm and allow them to walk on the snow without sinking.

# CHAPTER 5 | BEAUTIFUL FEATHERS

## The Cockatoo's Crest

The cockatoo is known for its beautiful crest. You can tell the mood of a cockatoo by looking at its crest. It opens the crest like a fan when it feels excited. It lays the crest back down when it feels calm.

In some bird **species**, the males have bright feathers, and the females have dull feathers. The male's bright feathers help him attract a mate. The female's colors help her hide while she nests.

## Pink Flamingos

Adult flamingos have bright pink and red feathers, but baby flamingos are not so colorful. A flamingo starts out life with white or gray feathers. Over the next few years, the feathers turn pink.

The pink color comes from the shrimp and other creatures that flamingos eat. A flamingo's color can change from light pink to deep red, depending on what it eats.

## The Peacock's Tail

The peacock can spread its tail like a fan. When a peacock shakes his tail, the bright green and blue feathers shimmer in the sunlight.

Peacocks are always male. Females are called peahens, and babies are peachicks. Together, they are known as peafowl.

# GLOSSARY

**camouflage**
coloring that helps an animal hide

**contour**
shape or outline

**crest**
the decorative feathers at the top of a bird's head

**keratin**
a hard material that forms hair, nails, and feathers

**molting**
losing feathers

**predators**
animals that hunt

**preening**
cleaning feathers

**prey**
an animal that is hunted

**species**
a type of animal or plant